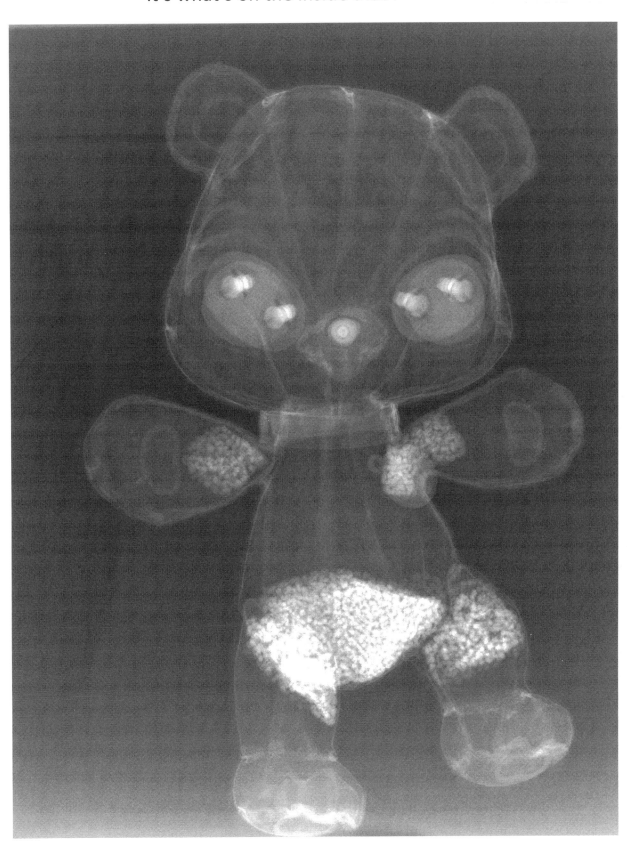

Publication Information

The Foreign Body: A collection of the most interesting X-rays of things that don't belong and the stories behind how they got there!

Andrew Del Gaizo, M.D.

Emergency Radiologist
Greensboro, N.C.

INTRODUCTION:

When I first tell people outside of the medical profession that I am an emergency radiologist, some variation of the following conversation often occurs:

Them: "So, you're the one that takes the x-rays of people? My friend/uncle/sister/former roommate is a radiologist too".

Me: "No, the hard working people who take the x-rays are the radiologic technologists. The radiologists like me are doctors behind the scenes, interpreting the x-rays and getting a report to your primary physician."

Them: "Oh, so you see all the x-rays? What's the craziest thing you've ever seen up someone's butt on an x-ray, or does that even really happen?"

Me: "You're referring to what we call a foreign body, and I've seen everything you can imagine... trust me, if it's out there, it's been in someone."

Now, as the reader, you may be questioning the sanity of the people I associate with and shocked by my response; *or*, perhaps you're pondering the rectal foreign body possibilities, certain that I underestimate the boundaries of your imagination. Either way, if you can't wait to find out, feel free to skip ahead to the XXX-rays.

For the rest of us, let's start with a couple definitions;

For·eign 'fȯr-ən': 1- alien in character: 2- occurring in an abnormal situation.
Bod·y 'bä-dē': a mass of matter distinct from other masses.

(As defined by the Merriam-Webster Dictionary, m-w.com)

When taken together;

Foreign Body: any object or substance found in an organ or tissue in which it does not belong under normal circumstances.

(As defined by Mosby's Medical Dictionary, 8th edition. © 2009, Elsevier)

Foreign bodies can be inserted, ingested, inhaled, or introduced (intentionally or by accident), and therefore can end up nearly anywhere within the body. From the skin surface, their position is often uncertain. However, x-rays can be used to detect a foreign body's location and decipher the best approach for removal.

This book will focus on foreign bodies that brought patients to emergency rooms. Prompt detection is often critical to minimizing complications. Therefore, all clinicians should be aware of what the various foreign bodies may look like on x-rays.

From the perspective of the general public, this book is written without complex medical terminology so that everyone can benefit from it. I'll show you the x-ray and let you guess what the foreign body is. Occasionally, I provide you with a clue to get started. But, as a picture is worth a thousand words, I'll often just let the image do the talking! On the subsequent page, I'll tell you what the foreign body was and how it got there. Often why it's there is as interesting as the image itself. Of course, all patient identifying information has been removed or changed to protect patient privacy and anonymity.

DISCLAIMER: The information provided in this book is for entertainment and educational purposes only, and should not be considered as offering medical advice. If you or someone you know may have a foreign body, please check with a qualified physician or other appropriate health care provider.

FOREIGN BODY CATEGORIES:

Category 1: Ingested or Inhaled

The mouth innocuously enough accepts foreign bodies. Unfortunately, there are tight areas within the gastrointestinal tract where these items can get stuck. Furthermore, some objects (such as sharp items or certain types of batteries) can be dangerous or toxic if not retrieved.   Inhaled foreign bodies are the ones that end up in the nose or airway, and in my experience, are most often the byproduct of turning your back for 2 seconds while your toddler explores the living room.

Category 2: Introduced

Welcome to the gun and knife show. Whether inadvertently caused by the patient or inflicted by someone else intending harm to the patient, x-rays play an important role in characterizing and localizing introduced foreign bodies. In addition to the medical relevance, these images often end up in forensics, delineating the type and trajectory of the weapon involved. We'll cover some of the ballistic basics as they pertain to x-rays in this section. The category also includes non-weapon foreign bodies that are introduced into the body, such as from stepping on a nail.

Category 3: Inserted

Last but not least…the XXX-rays. Technically, these foreign bodies could also be classified as introduced. However, given the "unique" circumstances under which many of these cases present, they deserve a category of their own. When activities occurring in the privacy of one's home go wrong, an embarrassing visit to the ER often ensues.

TABLE OF CONTENTS: Page

CATEGORY 1: INGESTED/INHALED

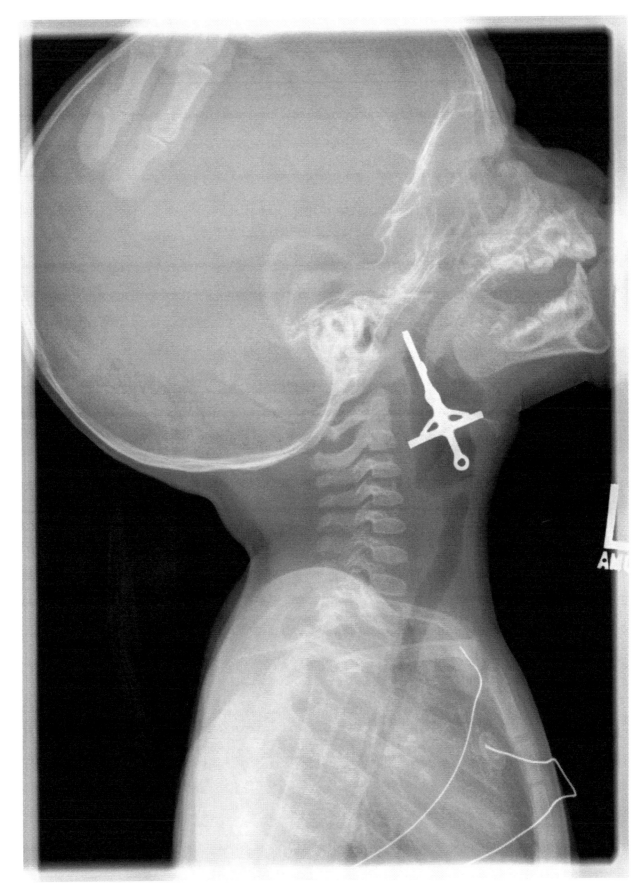

Crucifix

This little tyke was brought to the emergency room by his mother. He was drooling and demonstrating discomfort with swallowing. Mom wasn't sure what he had gotten a hold of, but was pretty sure he'd swallowed something. We took an x-ray and... found Jesus!

Clue: Pop Quiz

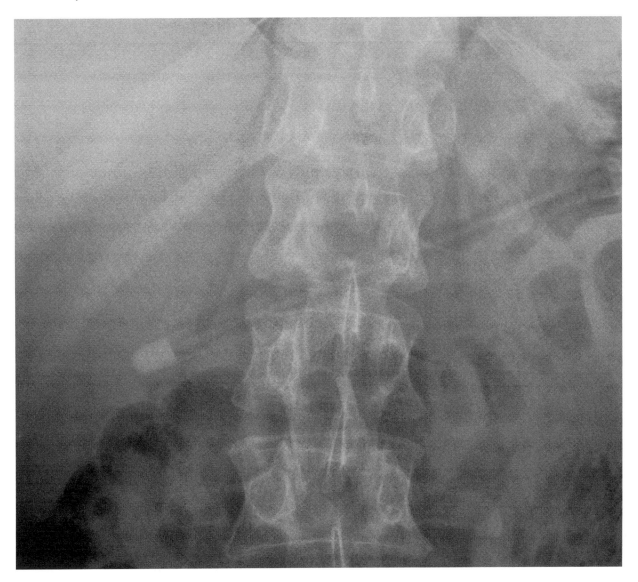

Pencil

Everyone take out your number 2 pencils.

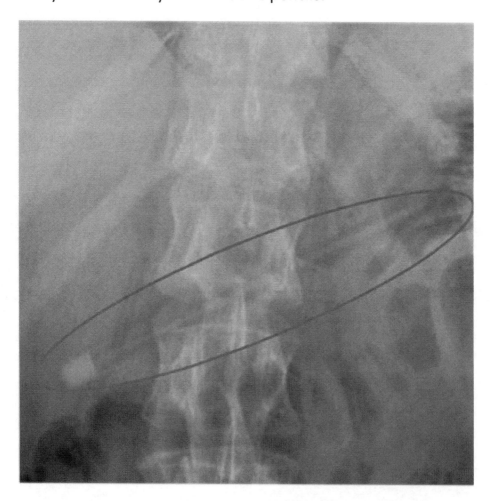

We see the metal ring that holds the eraser and if you look carefully, you also see a straight white line that represents the lead. The wood of the pencil is harder to see but takes the dark density of air. The eraser is invisible by x-ray.

Clue: Buffalo, NY's claim to fame

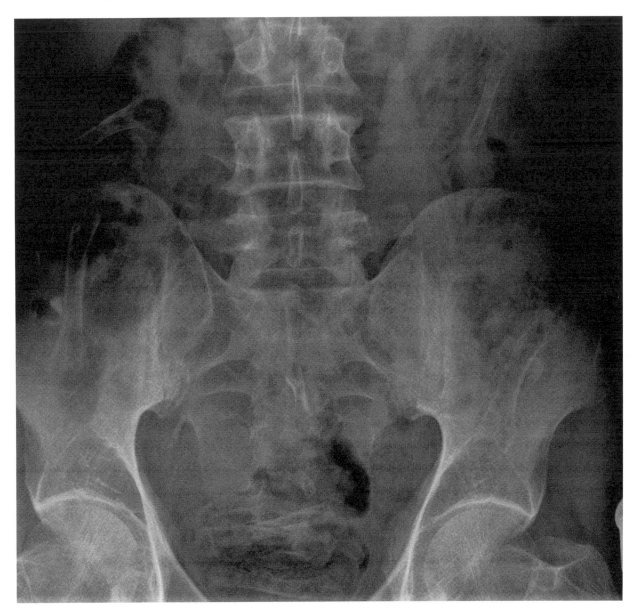

(Buffalo) chicken wing bones

A fraternity hot wing eating competition took an unusual twist for this pledge when he was informed that his dinner could be free if he'd just "clear his plate".

He was successful, bones and all, and here's the x-ray proof. I wonder if his frat brothers chipped in for his medical bill when he showed up in the ER a couple days later? For the record, chicken bones (usually swallowed by accident) are one of the most commonly ingested foreign bodies, and do occasionally cause bowel injury.

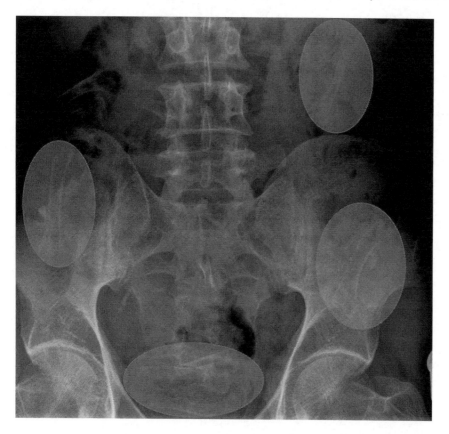

Here is the same x-ray, with circles around the chicken bones. Due to similarities in density, chicken bones can be quite subtle when they overly a patient's normal bones.

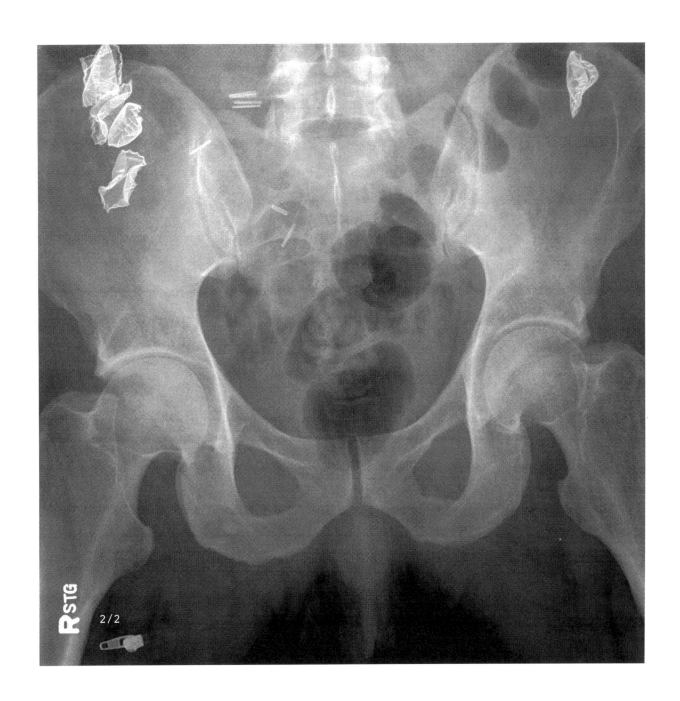

17

Bottle Caps

This guy liked to drink...a lot. He also had a habit of chewing on beer bottle caps. Sometimes, he'd pass out while still chewing on one. Occasionally, he'd wake up and the cap would be gone... We found them. The four on the right side had been there (stuck in part of the large intestines) over several prior x-rays (not shown). The one on the left was new.

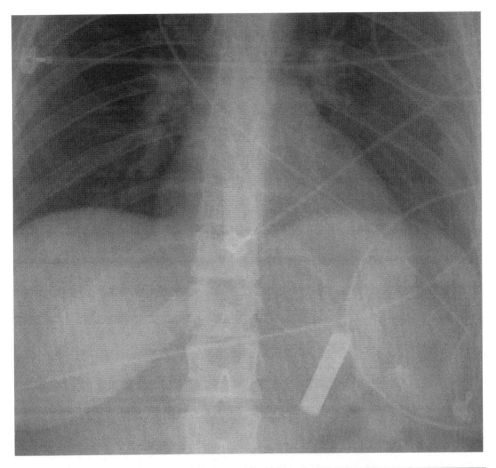

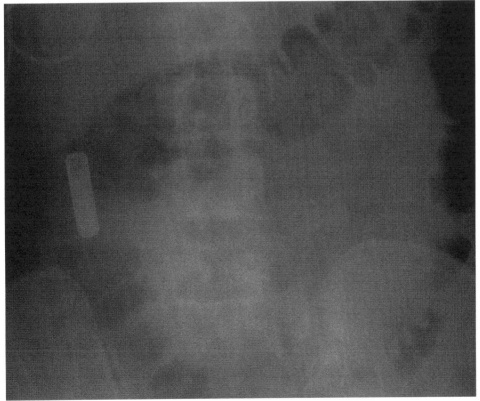

Double A batteries

There is some uncertainty in the community about the seriousness of a battery being swallowed. This most often occurs in children, and they should be brought to the emergency room immediately. If the battery is stuck in the esophagus, emergent removal will be necessary. If the battery has already reached the intestines, observation is the most common management.

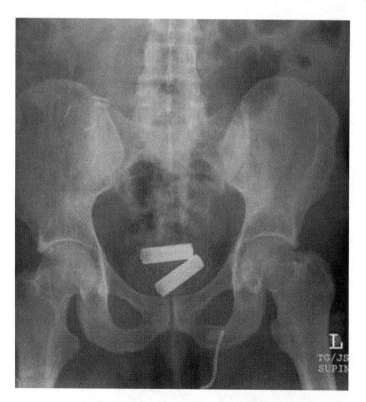

Our patient swallowed 2 batteries and by the time the x-ray was performed, they had already reached the colon. Therefore, the decision was made to observe and intervene only if the batteries didn't keep moving. Fortunately, an x-ray the next morning (above) showed both batteries had reached the rectum and were "removed" naturally after her morning coffee.

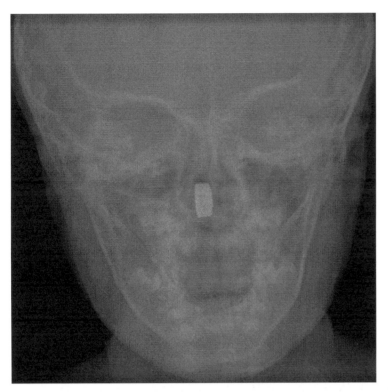

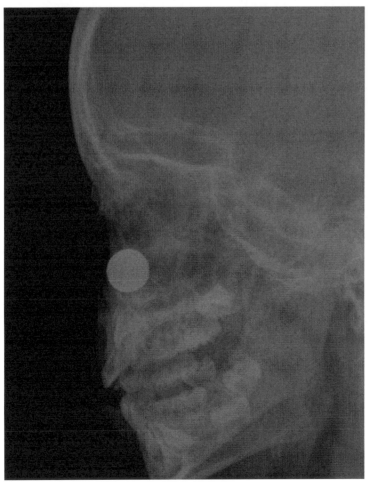

Button Battery

To all the moms out there, you're not alone if your kid has done something like this. It is common for young children to place foreign bodies in their ears or nose. Unfortunately, sometimes they get stuck. Button batteries can cause a serious alkaline reaction if not promptly removed.

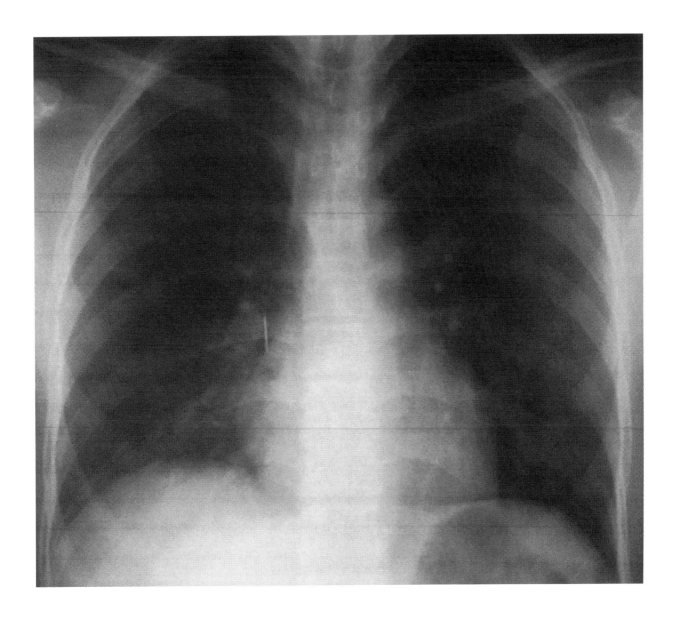

Finishing Nail

Think this could never happen to you? You may have been closer than you think! Standing on a ladder, about to hang a picture on the wall; got the nail in one hand, reach for the hammer with the other. Now I'll just get the picture... uh oh, all out of hands. No big deal, I'll hold the nail in my mouth for a second and then... gulp!

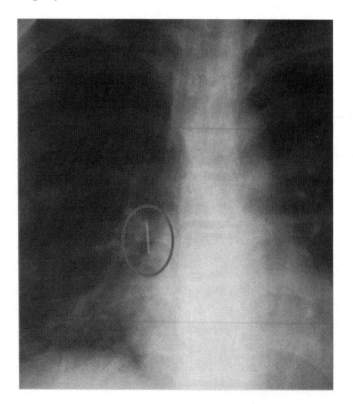

This guy was installing crown molding, but you get the point. Unfortunately, the nail fell into his bronchus (air pipe) supplying the right lung. Fortunately, the pulmonologist was able to retrieve it and the patient did fine.

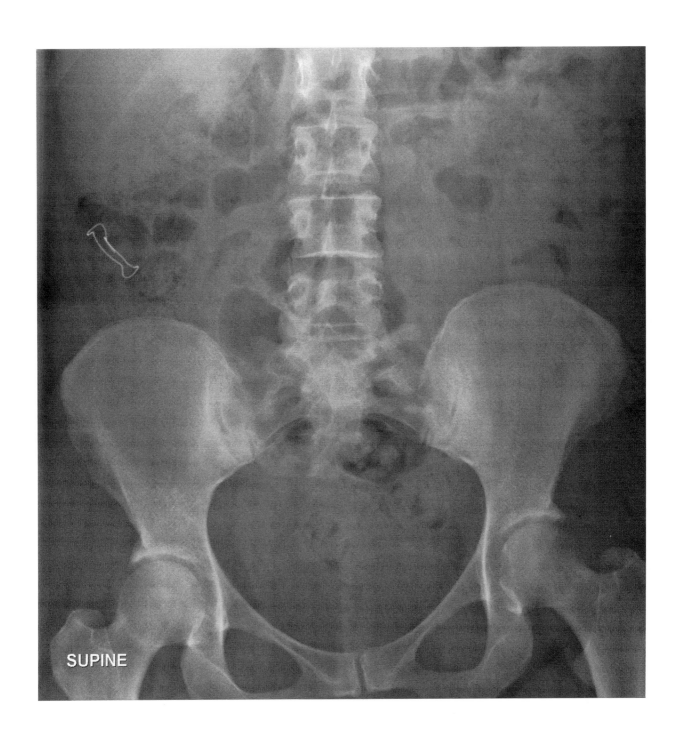

SUPINE

Retainer (bottom teeth)

Mom asked Junior where his retainer was. He said it disappeared while he was sleeping. Knowing he hated to wear it, she planned to ground him for losing it (or throwing it out again as he had done at school the week before when he left it on his lunch tray).

But Junior was insistent, so she brought him in to see us. Sure enough, there it was. As expected, the plastic doesn't show up on the x-ray so we just see the metal part. At this point, we waited for it to pass on its own.

I'm still not sure if Junior swallowed his retainer on accident or if he is an evil genius. After "passing" the retainer, mom *insisted* he throw it away this time!

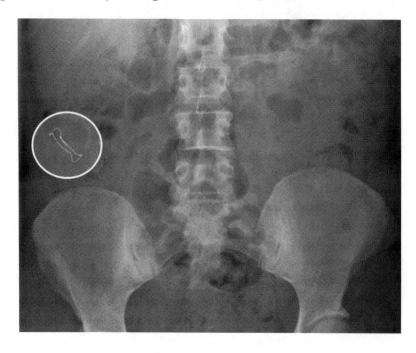

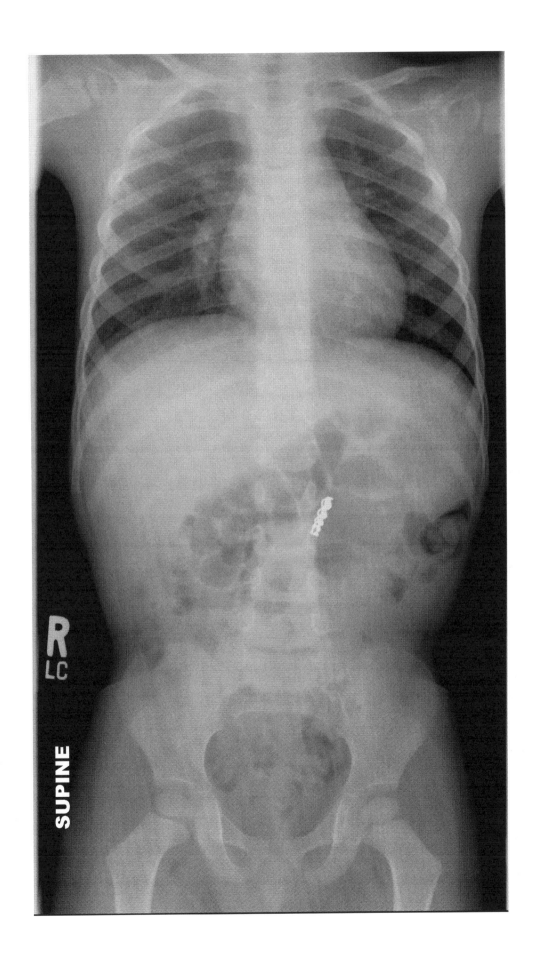

Earring

It is so common for kids to swallow foreign bodies, that we've customized an x-ray that covers the lungs and entire gastrointestinal tract on one picture (as above). In this case, mom saw her child swallow the earring. More often, parents probably don't even know where that missing earring is. When the sharp part is not exposed (as in this case), small earrings tend to pass on their own and require no intervention.

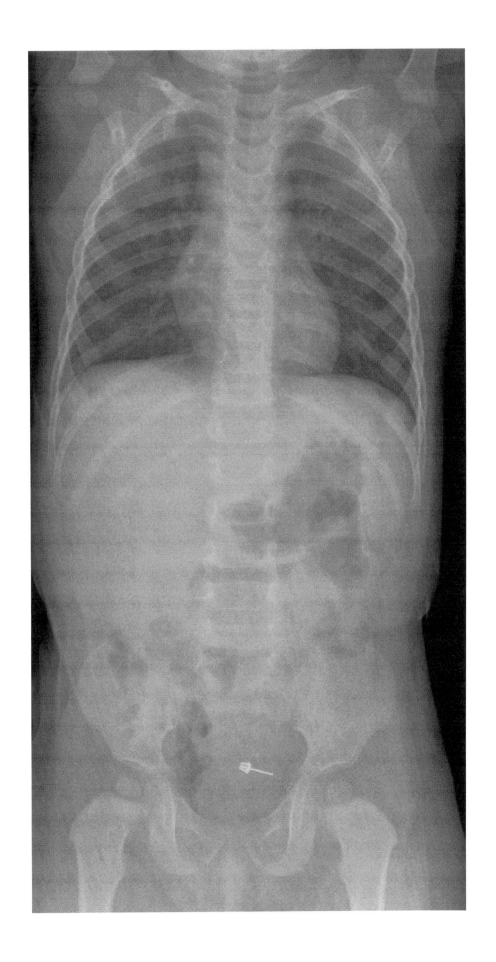

Earring

The post of this diamond earring was found in a different patient using the full body search for foreign body x-ray described above. In this case, it had already reached the colon, and was allowed to pass without intervention.

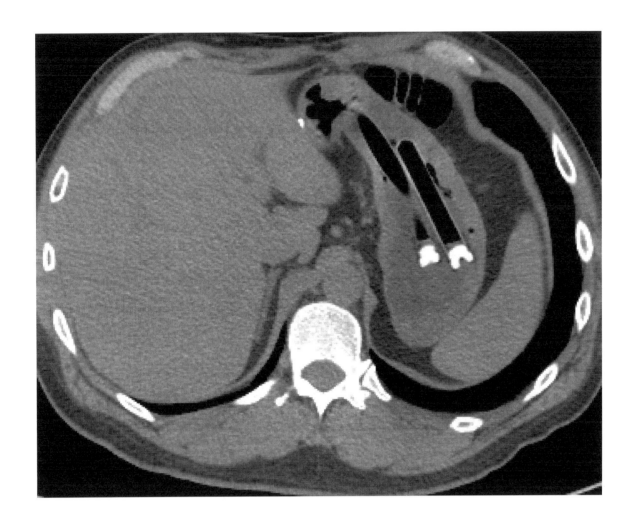

Test Tubes

Pica is a condition in which there is consumption of items of no nutritional value. While being evaluated for this condition, the doctor asked the patient what the last substance was that she had swallowed. Pointing at a row of tubes used to collect samples that were on the counter in the examining room, the patient admitted to swallowing a couple while waiting for the doctor...

The next stop was the emergency room, where we did a CAT scan and found the tubes in her stomach. See how dark the insides are? That's air within the empty tubes. Due to their size we were concerned about whether the tubes would make it all the way through without getting stuck somewhere in the intestines. Therefore, the decision was made to have a gastroenterologist place a scope in through the patient's mouth, reach into the stomach, and retrieve the tubes out.

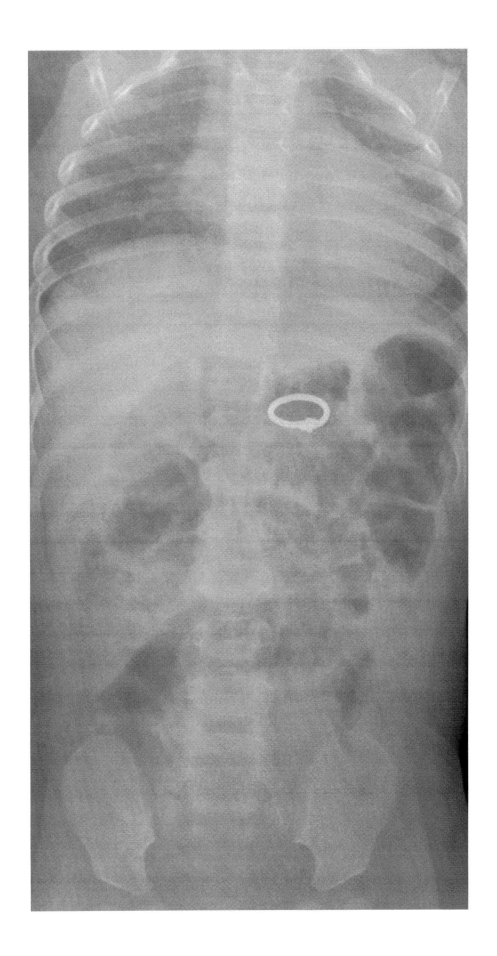

Wedding Ring

What's worse than that feeling you get when you think you've lost your wedding ring? Realizing your son may have just eaten it is probably worse... In this case, we spotted the ring in the baby's stomach and were able to retrieve it. The boy did fine, and mom renewed her vows never to take it off again!

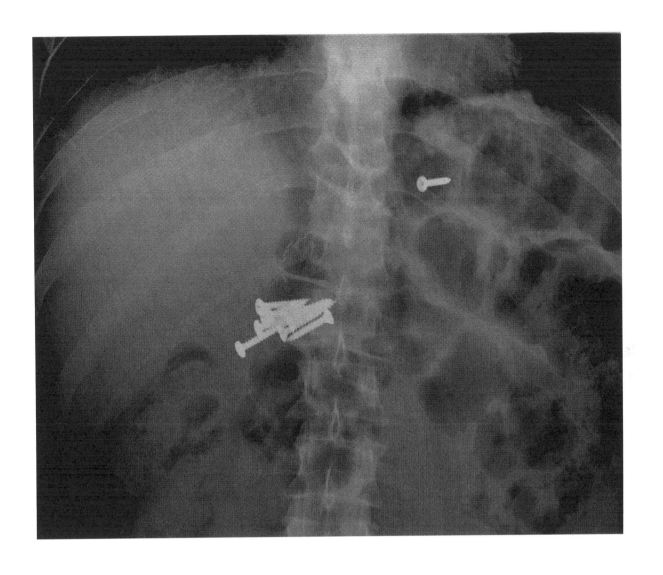

Screws

In contrast to our patient earlier, who inadvertently inhaled a nail into his lungs, this patient was intentionally swallowing screws. The patient had a history of swallowing metal objects and refused surgery or intervention. Anecdotally, the weight of the screw heads seemed to lead the screws through the intestines head first and the screws passed without complication. Despite this observation, swallowing screws is NOT recommended!

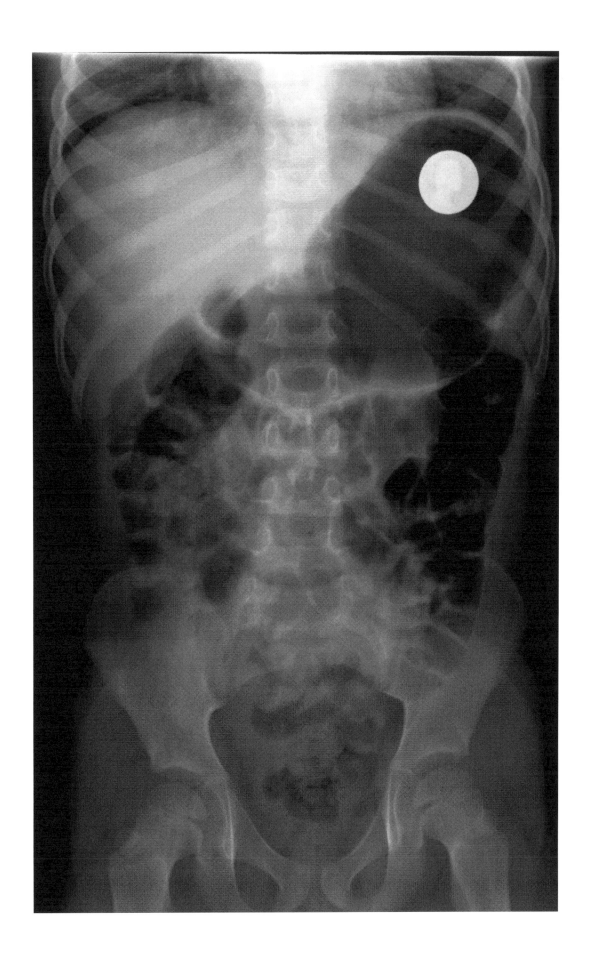

Coin-Quarter

If I had a quarter for every time a kid swallowed a quarter...

Not sure why, maybe it's the shape, maybe it's the shine, but kids love to swallow coins. Let's be honest, does it really make sense to have coins as currency anymore? I mean, almost nothing costs less than a dollar. But I digress. Here are a few more coin x-rays.

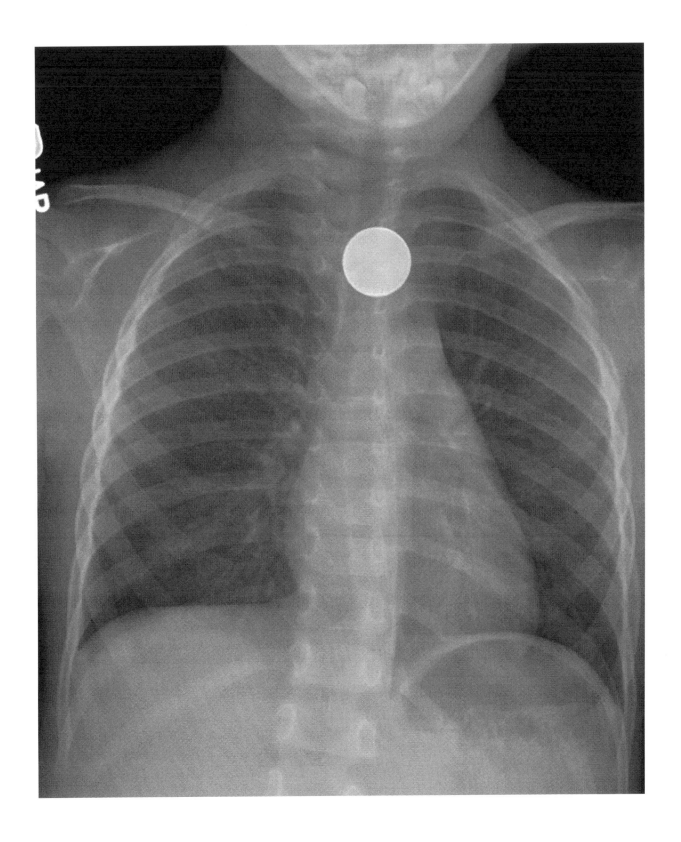

Coin-Penny

Can we at least get rid of the penny? The coin looks relatively big as compared to the last case because this patient was much younger (and smaller).

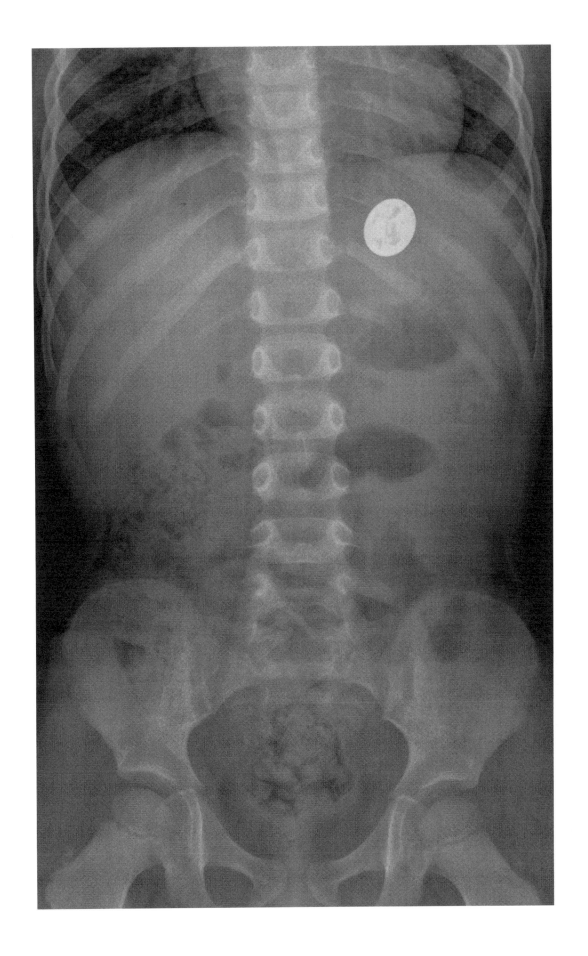

Coin-Nickel

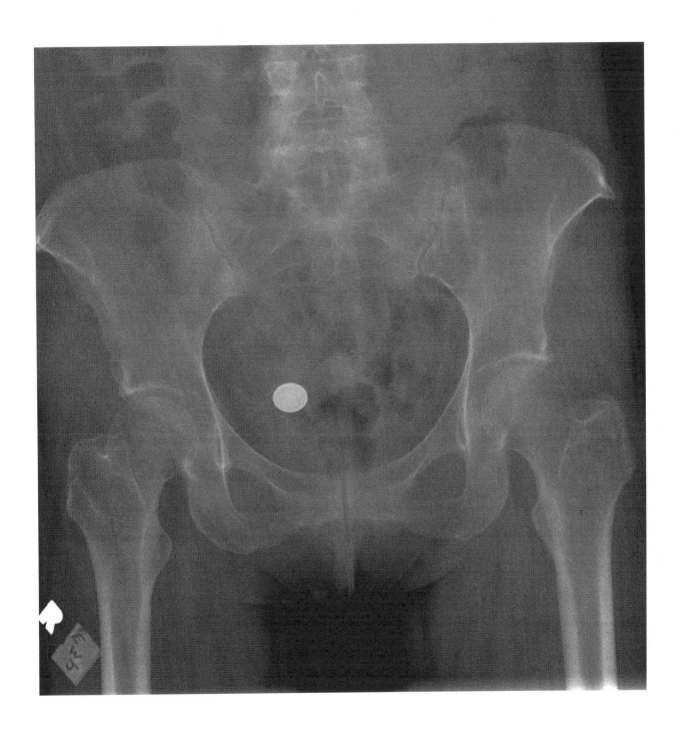

Coin-Dime

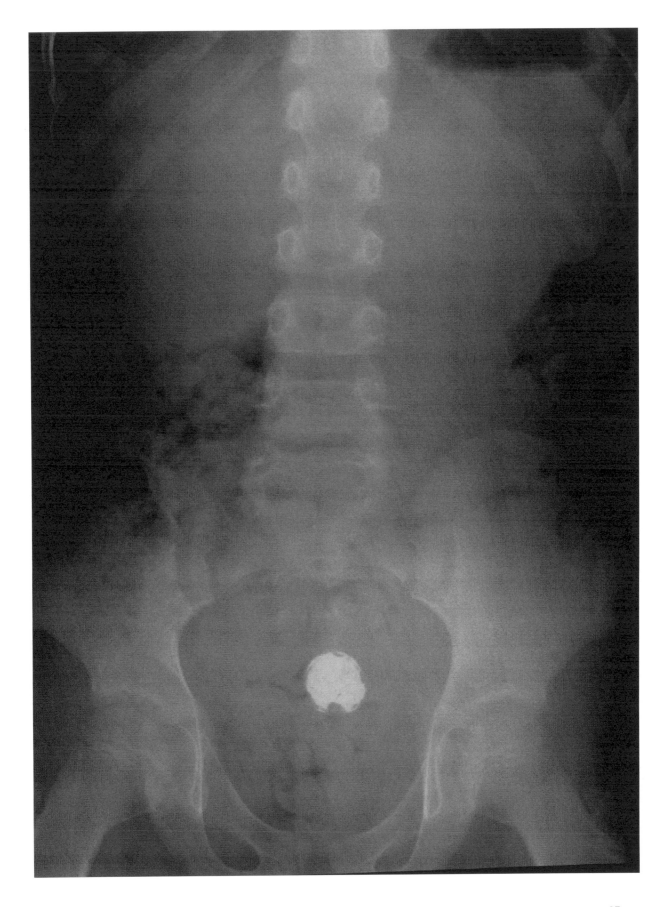

Coin-Flattened Penny

Apparently even the novelty flattened pennies from Disneyland are delicious...

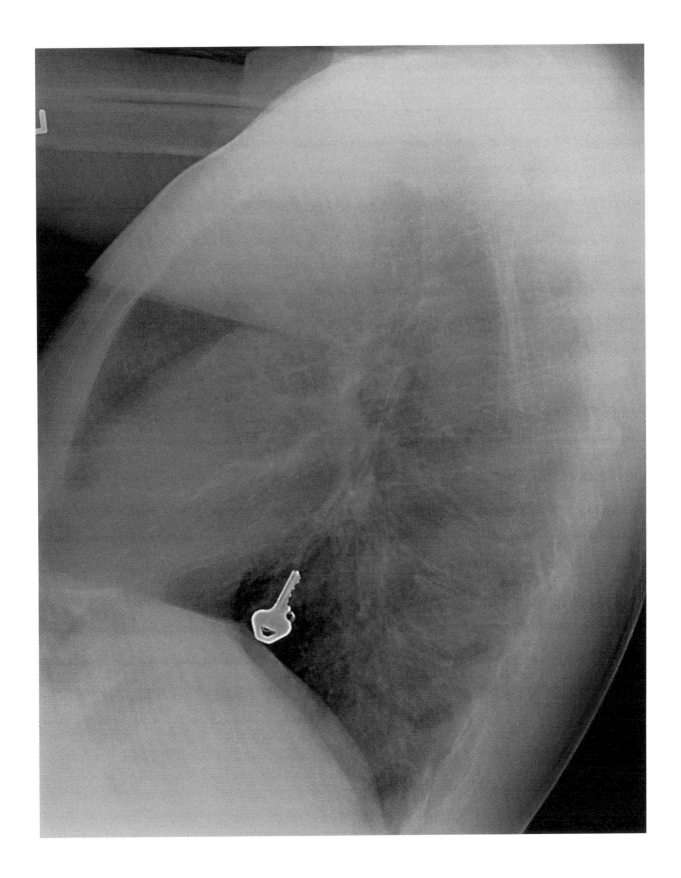

Key

Another commonly misplaced household item turns up inside the body of a patient. This one is stuck in the esophagus and had to be retrieved.

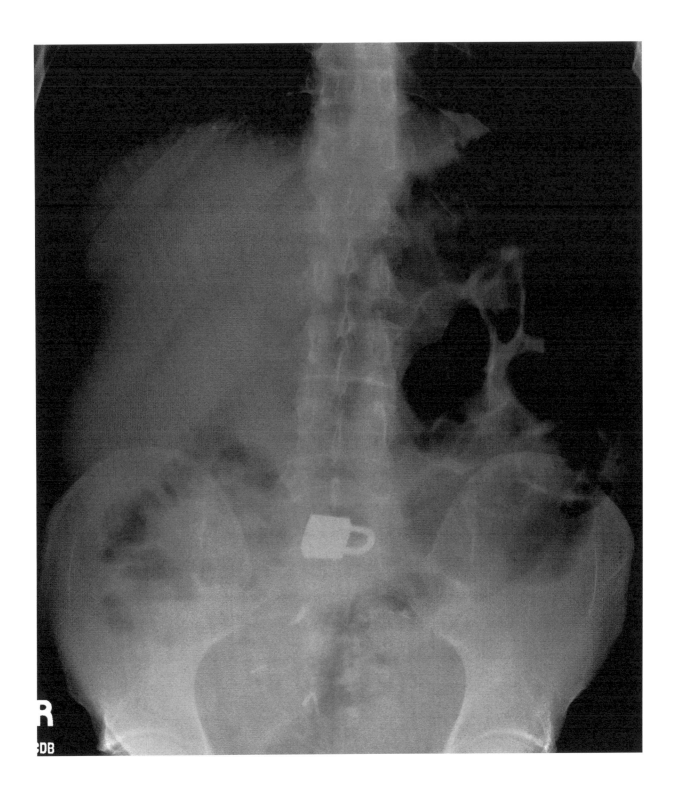

R

CDB

Luggage Lock

They come with every suitcase I have ever purchased, but does anyone actually use these things? Either way, these tiny locks make the perfect ingestible foreign body.

CATEGORY 2: INTRODUCED

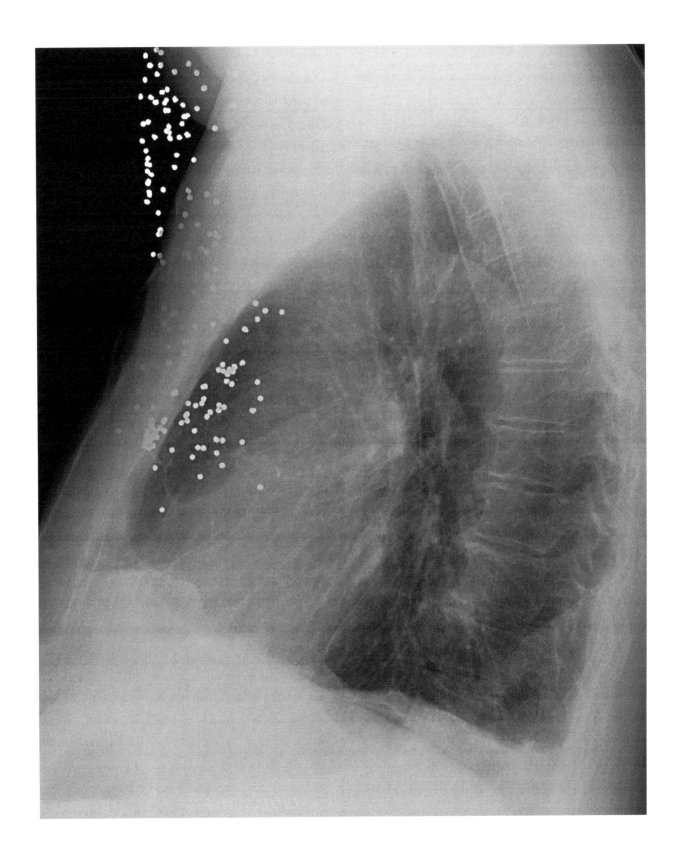

Birdshot

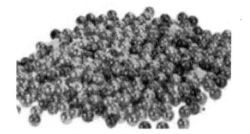

This is what you look like after hunting with Dick Cheney. Actually, this patient presented to the ER with a cough. We asked about the bullets lodged in his right chest wall and arm, and he acknowledged being shot a few years prior. He said he hasn't been able to walk through a metal detector without setting it off since.

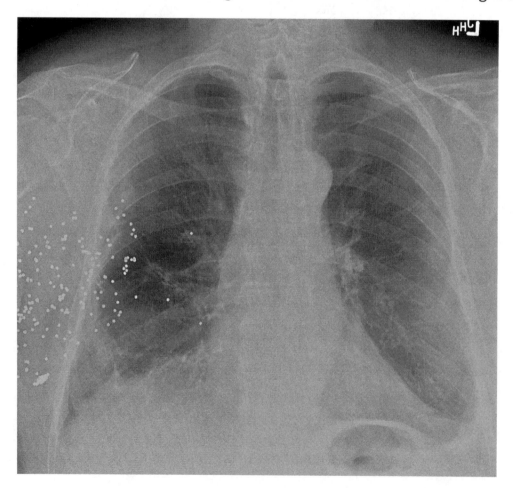

This is the same patient from the front.

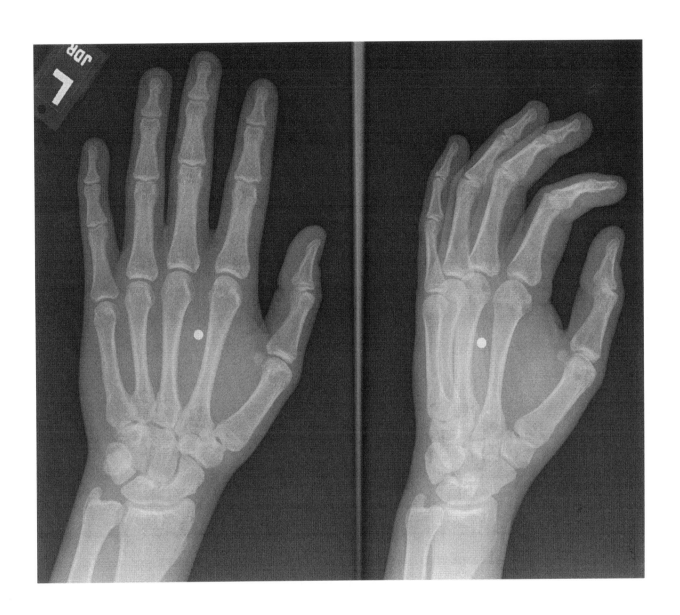

Birdshot

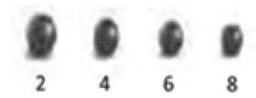

This pellet is larger than those seen on the prior case. American standard birdshot gets larger as the number gets lower.

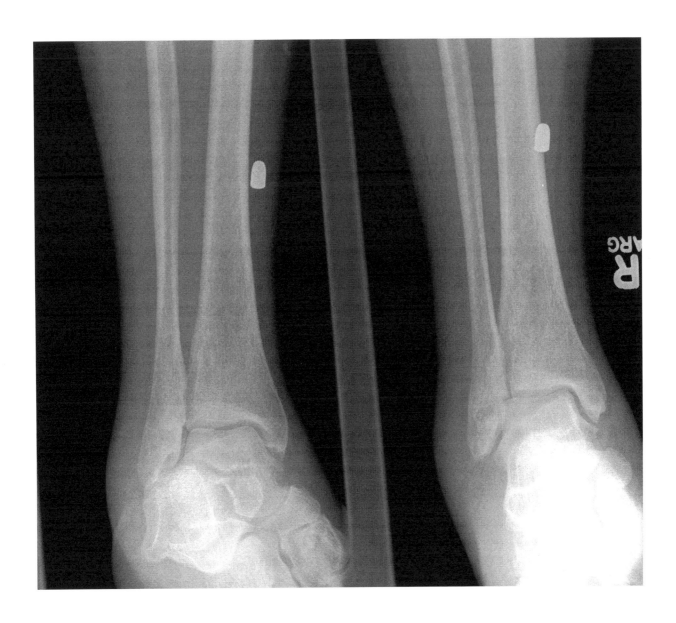

Bullet: Solid Point, Fully Jacketed 9-mm

Gauging bullet type and caliber by x-ray can be tricky. However, the degree of bullet fragmentation can give us a clue as to the bullet construction. Bullets with full metal jackets as in this case often remain in one piece and tend not to deform or leave a trail of fragments.

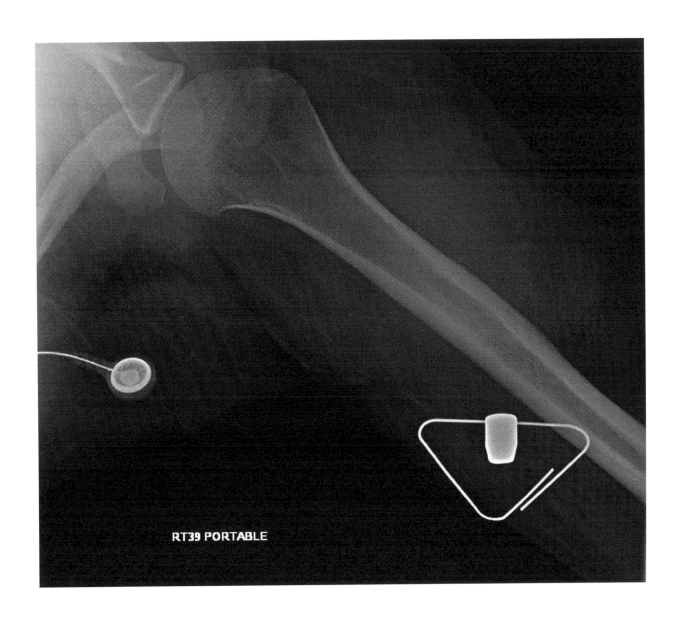

RT39 PORTABLE

Bullet: (Jacketed) Hollow Point

This is the x-ray of a patient's arm, close to his shoulder joint. The triangle shaped paperclip is placed on the patient's skin so that we know where the bullet entered. Not too far from that site is the bullet. Hollow points tend to expand on impact though the jacket limits the amount of expansion. However, this bullet maintained its shape as contact occurred at a relatively slow velocity. The bull lodged within the muscles and never contacted bone.

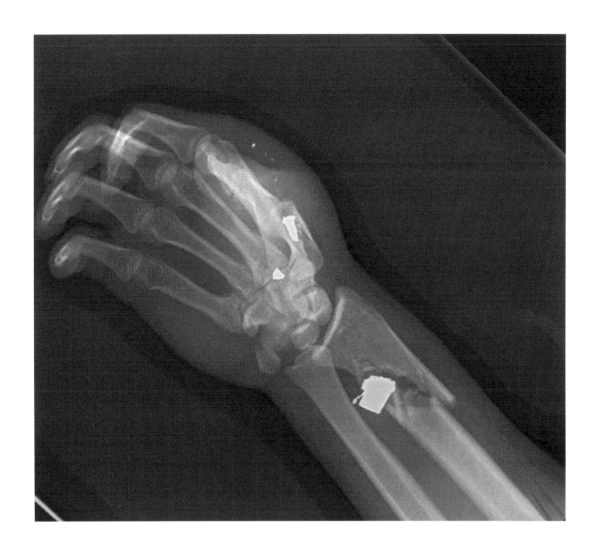

Bullet: Hollow-point, Semi-jacketed

In contrast, this x-ray shows the characteristic mushrooming of semi-jacketed and hollow-point bullets, which tend to deform on impact. There can be mild bullet fragmentation.

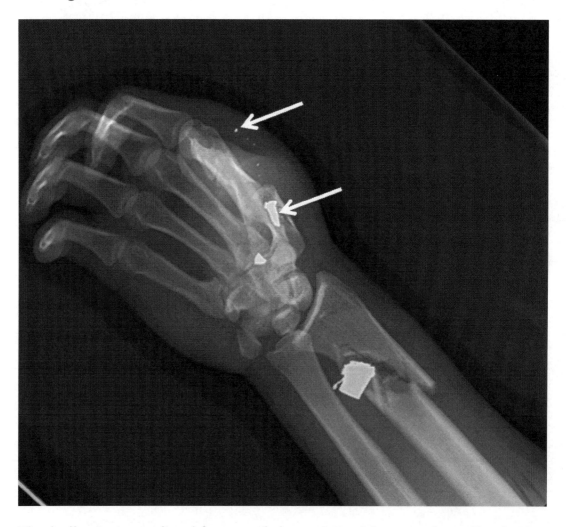

The bullet impacted and fractured the wrist, with several smaller fragments (arrows) traveling into and fracturing bones of the thumb.

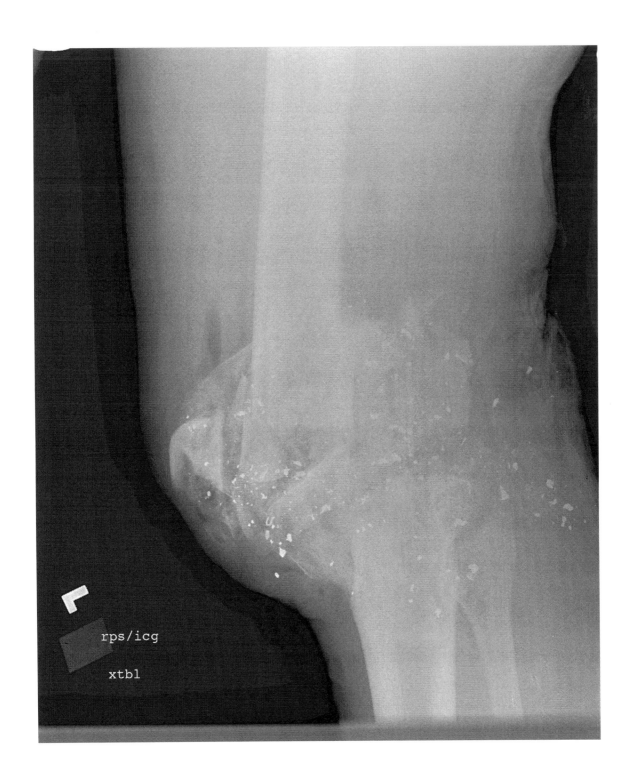

rps/icg

xtbl

Bullet: Soft Point Rifle

High-velocity soft-point rifle bullets usually undergo marked fragmentation on impact, creating a lead snowstorm that no longer resembles the original round. The fragment spread widens as the distance from the entry site increases, with the apex pointing toward the entry site.

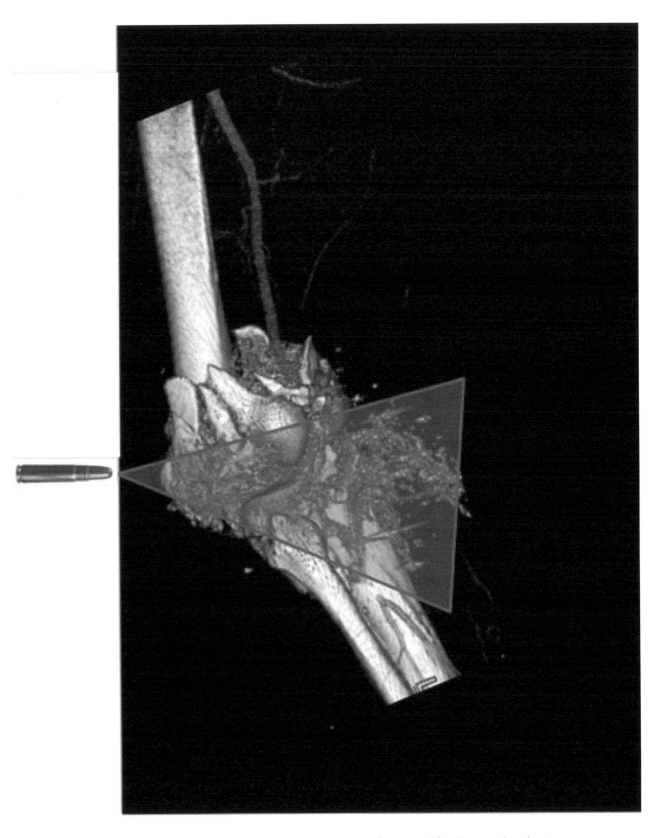

Notice the widening of fragments behind the knee (triangle). The red tube is the artery supplying the leg, which was disrupted.

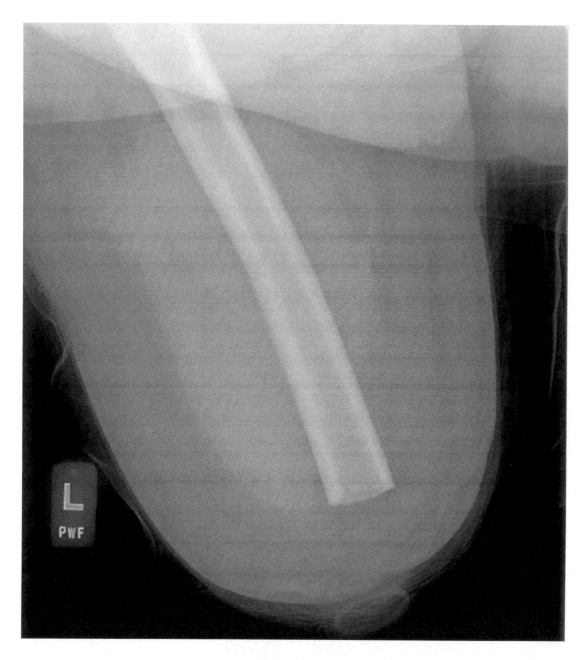

Unfortunately, the patient's leg had to be amputated.

References for the "bullet" cases:

1. Wilson AJ. Gunshot Injuries: What Does a Radiologist Need to Know? September 1999 RadioGraphics, 19, 1358-1368.

2. Dimaio VJM. Gunshot wounds: practical aspects of firearms, ballistics, and forensic techniques Boca Raton, Fla: CRC Press, 1985; 163-226, 257–265.

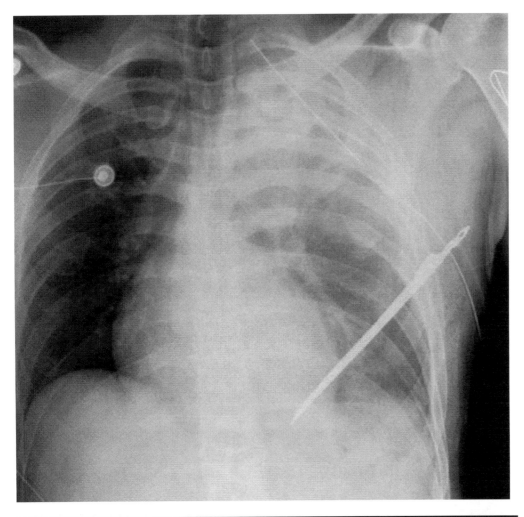

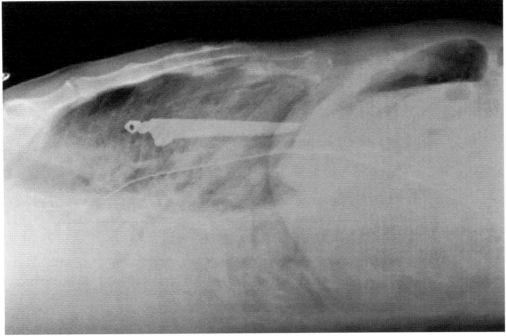

Kitchen Knife

This was a domestic dispute gone bad. Notice how we only see the metal part of the knife on the x-ray? The handle was sticking out of the patient, but was made of plastic. Most types of plastic don't show up on x-ray.

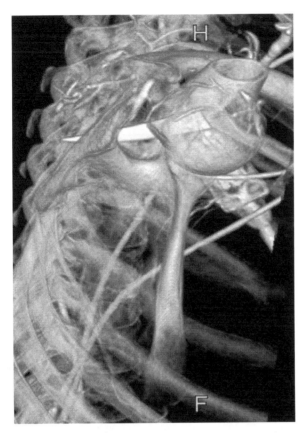

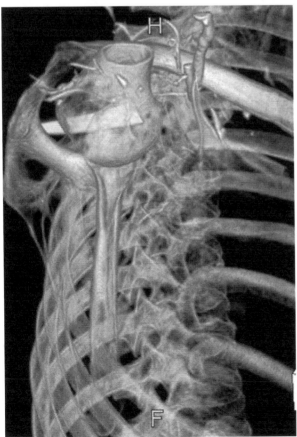

Knife

In this case, 3-D reformatted images were obtained to help us define exactly where the knife went in preparation for surgical removal. The blade pierced the muscles near the shoulder joint and above the shoulder blade (scapula).

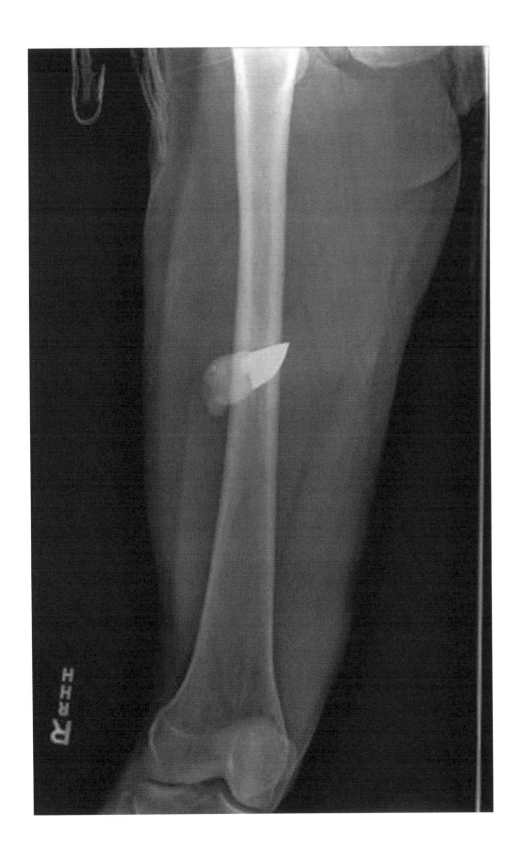

Knife

In the leg...scary view of the blade comin' at ya.

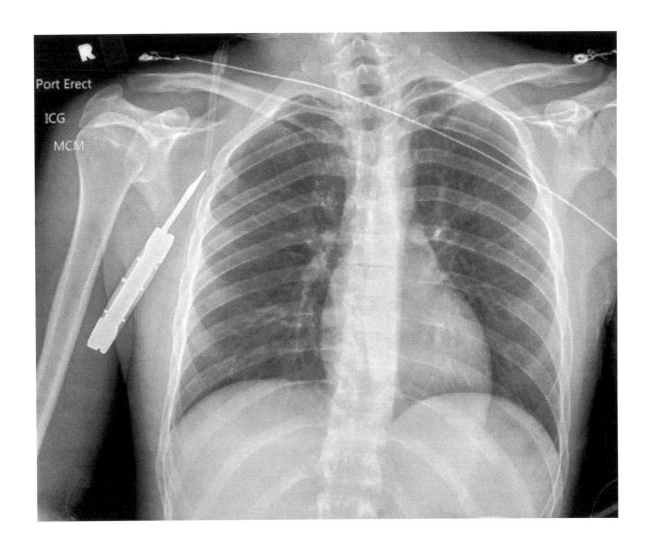

Pocket Knife

You call that a knife?

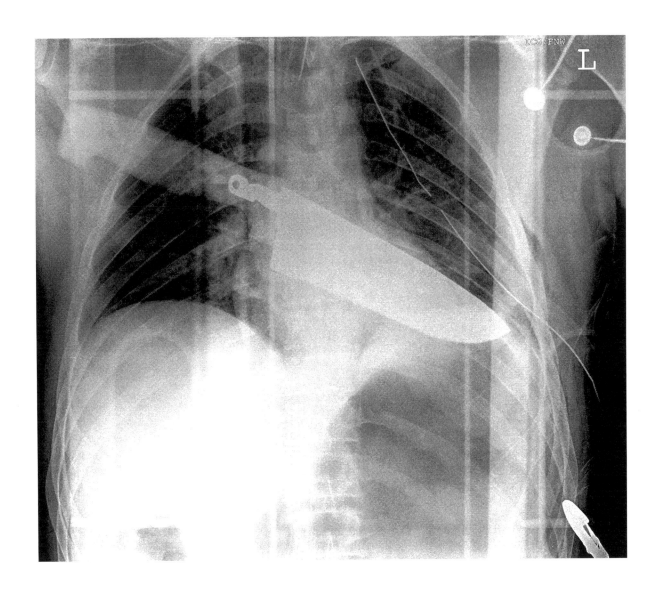

Butcher Knife

This is a knife.

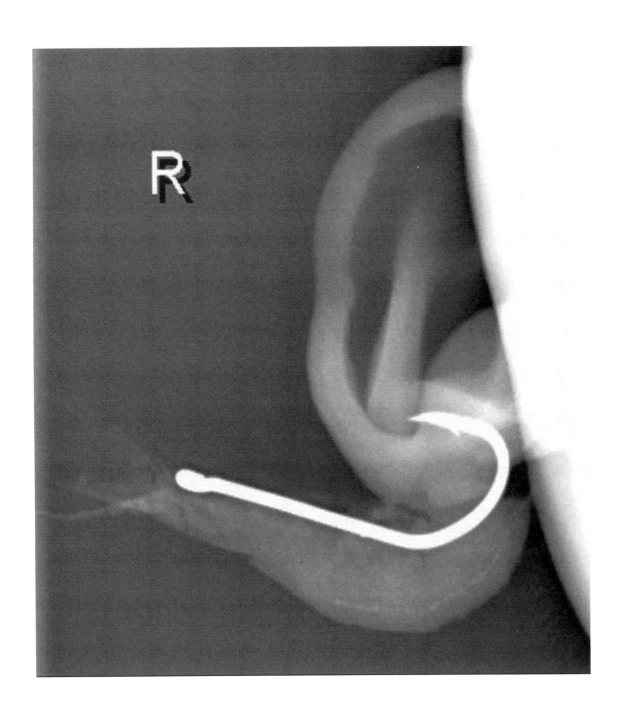

Fishhook

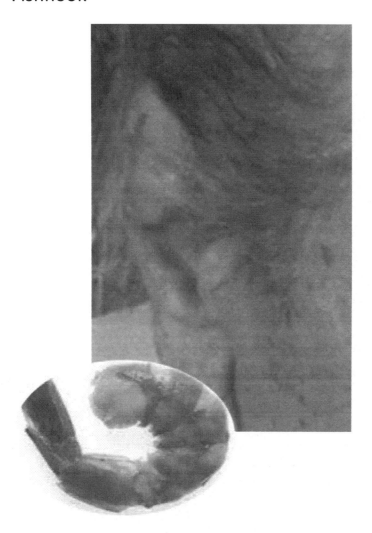

A man's fishing trip didn't quite go as planned. Lodged in his right ear is a fishing hook attached to a headless shrimp that was being used as bait. Revenge perhaps?

Above is my sophisticated artistic rendering of what the ER docs saw when the fisherman showed up. (I know what you're thinking...stick to x-rays Del Gaizo!)

Case courtesy of Dr. Andrew Dixon Alfred Health / Imaging @ Olympic Park, Melbourne, Australia. Reprinted with permission from http://radiopaedia.org/cases/hook-with-prawn-in-pinna.

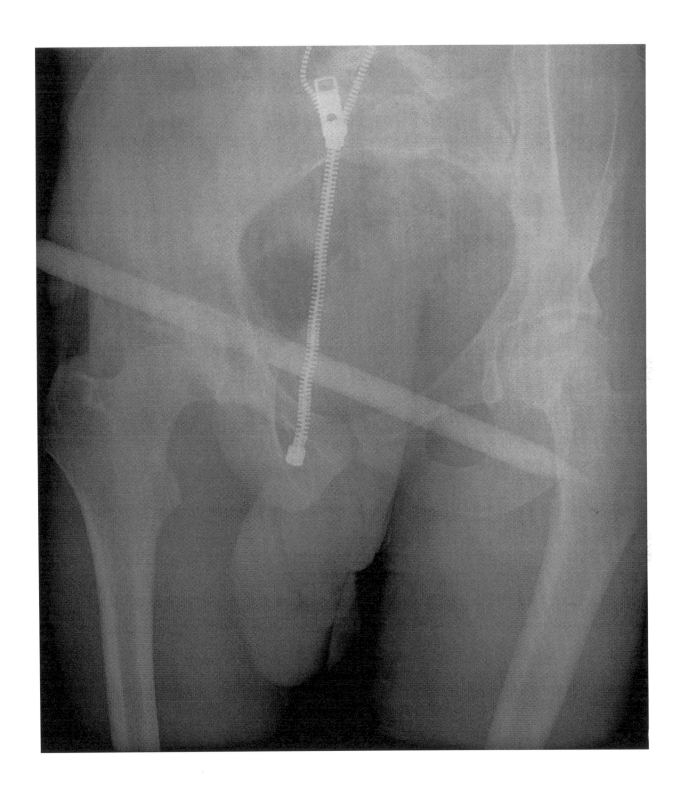

Ground Rod

When construction sites go wrong. You're seeing about 2 feet of this 6 foot long grounding rod on the x-ray. The rest was sticking out of the patient.

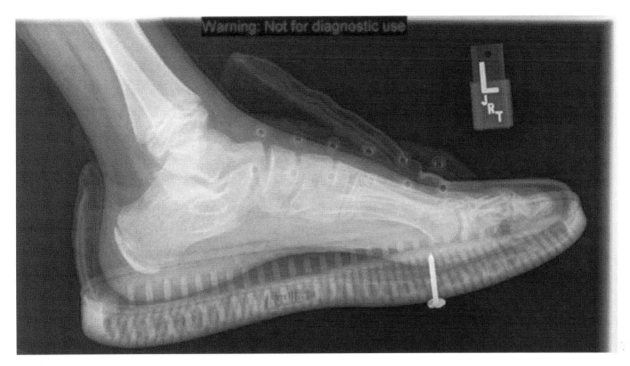

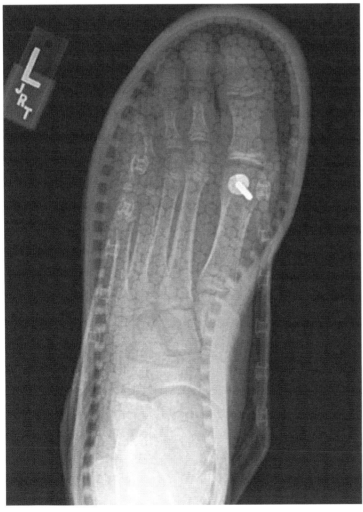

Nail

What started off as record time for "Ned" during his half marathon training turned into a marathon of waiting in the emergency room... all because of one ill-fated step.

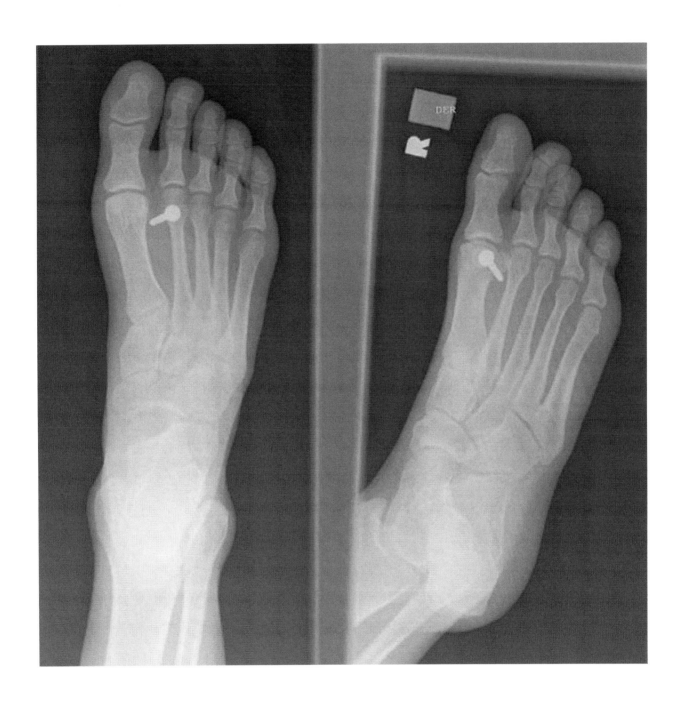

S.I.F.

S.I.F. is a well-known acronym that stands for screw- in- foot.

Okay, you got me; I just made that acronym up. But, this is your clue for the xxx-ray S.I.P. case later in the book.

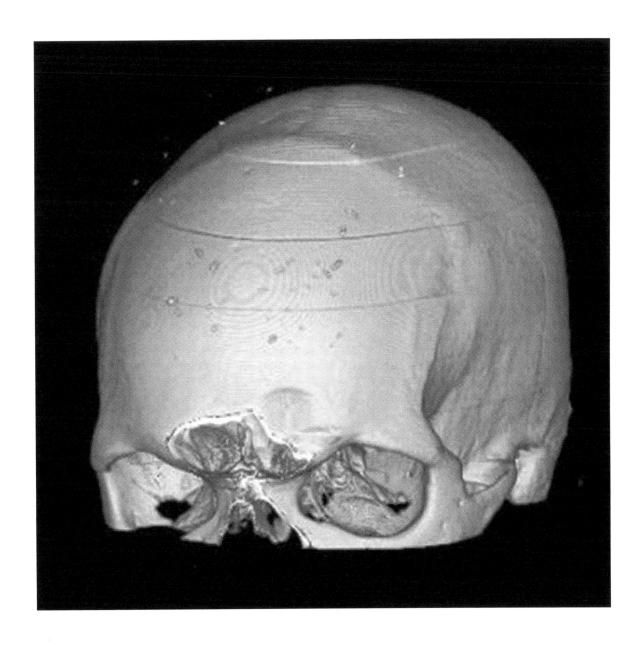

Glass pebbles

This patient was fortunate in that he sustained no serious injuries following a motor vehicle collision. This 3-D reformatted image demonstrates numerous pebbles of glass embedded in his scalp, corresponding to the shattered tempered glass of the driver side window.

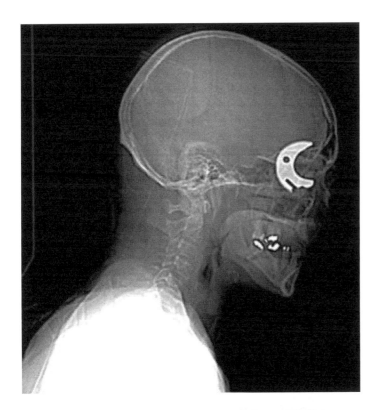

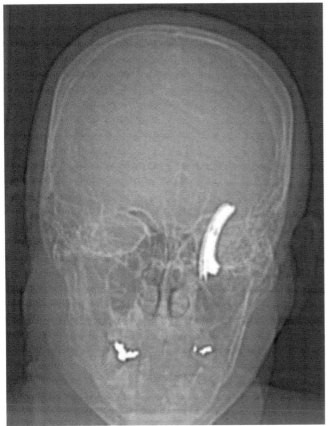

Blade

Part II of when construction sites go wrong. This finger joint cutting blade broke off while cranking at 7200 RPM. While there's no saving the eye in this scenario, he otherwise made a full recovery.

CATEGORY 3: INSERTED

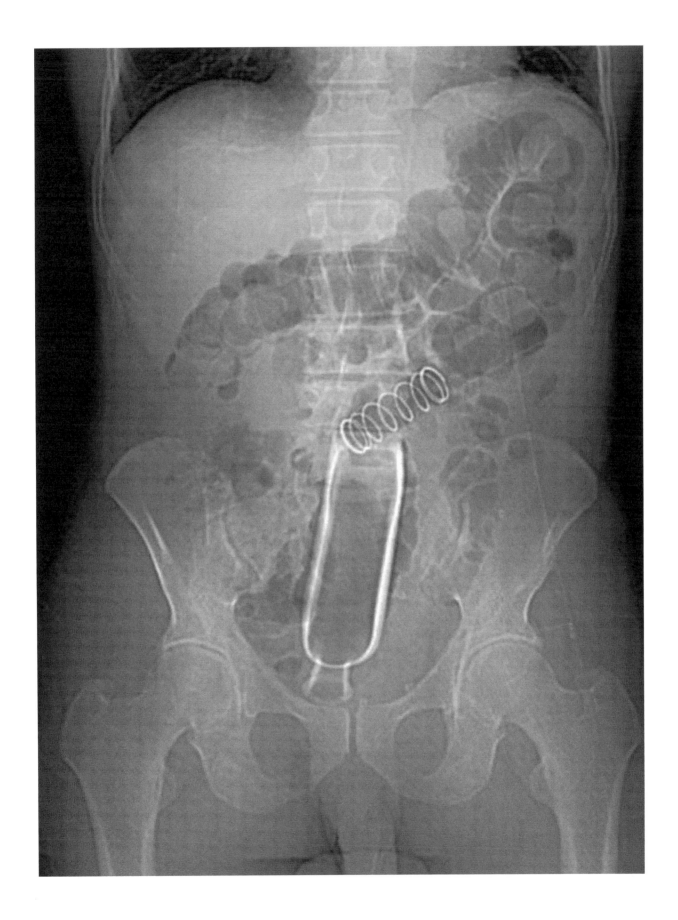

Toilet Paper Spindle/Holder and Shampoo Bottle

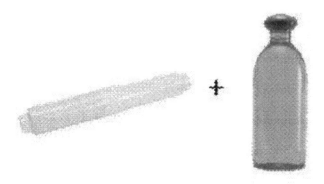

The patient provided history was fell in the shower, landed on a shampoo bottle. Sounds like a million to one shot, but we gave the patient the benefit of the doubt.

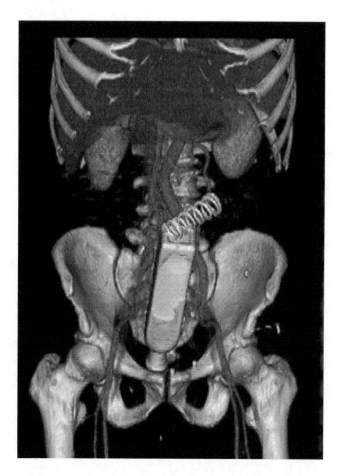

However, when we got the x-ray, apparently he must have fallen twice, as a toilet paper spindle was also present. Some plastics don't show up on x-ray, which is why we only see the metal spring of the spindle.

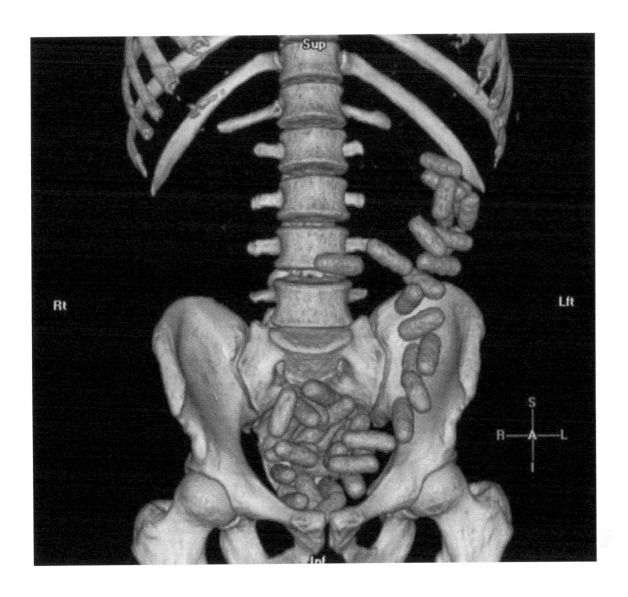

Sup

Rt

Lft

S
R — A — L
I

93

Body Packer/Drug Mule

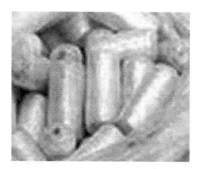

This patient was traveling from South America and arrested by police officers at the airport for strange behavior. The interrogation confirmed the man to be a body packer (where pellets or balloons of illicit drugs are ingested or inserted for illegal transport). The strange behavior raised suspicion for rupture of one of the packets. There was no rupture, so apparently he always behaves strangely when walking around with 500g of cocaine in his colon... Go figure.

Case courtesy of Dr. Stefan Götschi, Switzerland. Reprinted with permission from http://radiopaedia.org/cases/body-packer-1.

Clue: Dentist recommended, twice a day

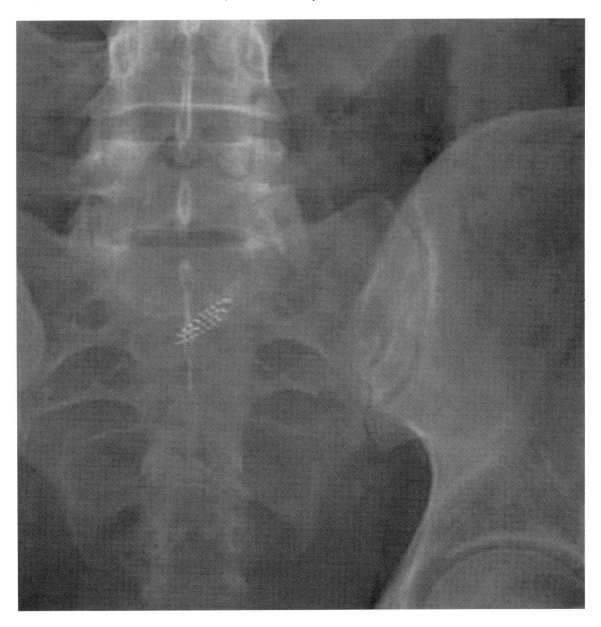

Toothbrush

Four out of 5 dentists agree, don't insert a toothbrush into your rectum...Wait, does that mean 1 in 5 prefer it!?

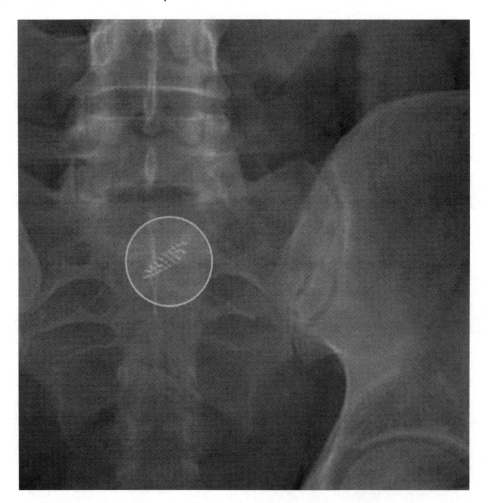

Notice how the plastic handle is invisible on x-ray. We just see the bristles (circle).

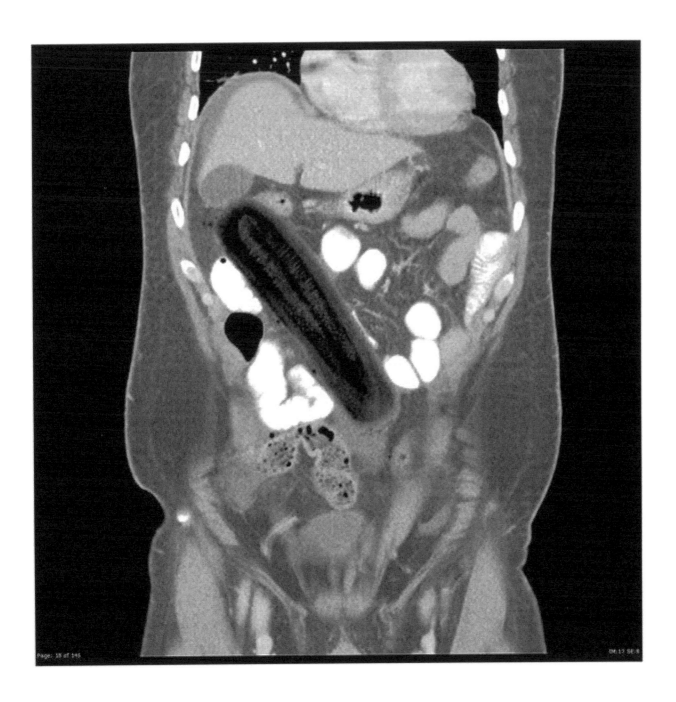

Zucchini

This case of a zucchini is particularly unusual as it ruptured out of the bowel and was freely floating in the abdominal cavity. This does raise questions as to how hard one has to push a blunt vegetable to tear entirely through the rectum!

Case courtesy of Dr. Frank Gaillard, Royal Melbourne Hospital, Melbourne, Australia. Reprinted with permission from http://radiopaedia.org/cases/intraperitoneal-zucchini.

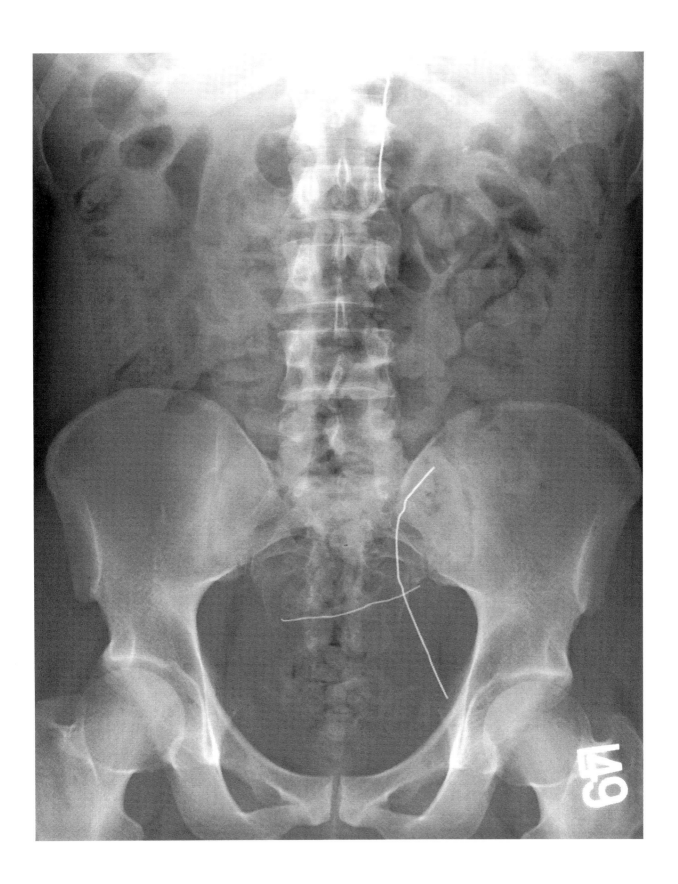

Paperclips

In prison, anything can become a weapon (or perhaps a lock pick?).This inmate was at an offsite work assignment when an astute guard noted the inmate held several paperclips in his mouth. Perhaps because he became symptomatic, the prisoner admitted to "concealing" 2 additional clips down below. Therefore, the guard brought him to the hospital for evaluation.

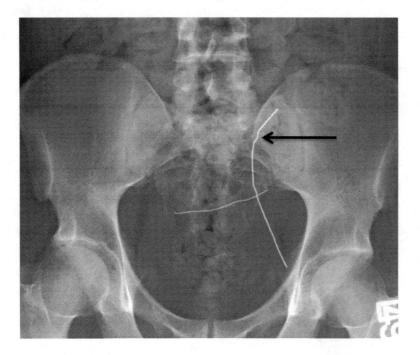

The guard's decision turned out to be fortuitous for the prisoner. While one of the paperclips was in the rectum, the other (arrow) had pierced the bowel wall and would have been a risk for serious complications. This was confirmed by the presence of abdominal air outside of bowel (not shown).

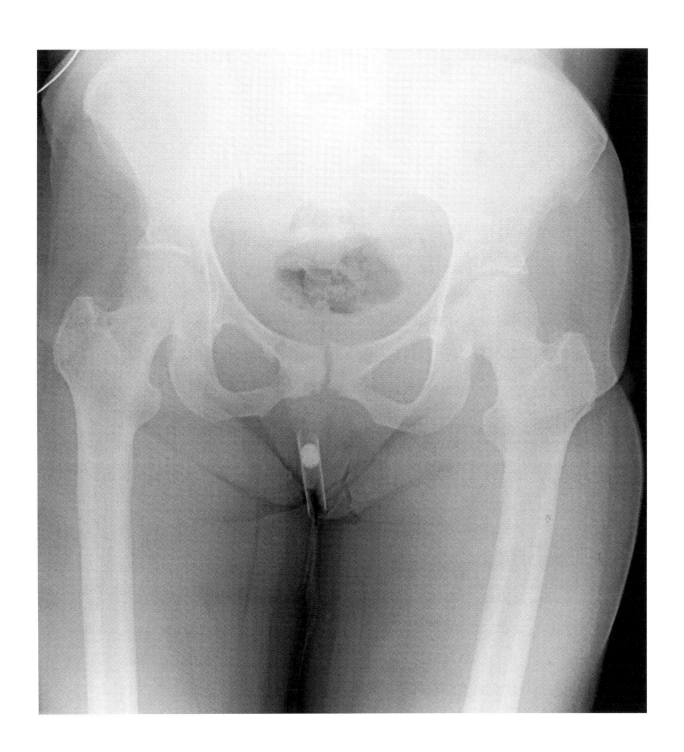

Crack Pipe in the Vagina

Crack is wack. This woman claimed not to be under the influence following a motor vehicle crash. The good news: no bone fractures. The bad news: next stop, jail. Pipe image courtesy of http://www.enterprisemobilitymatters.com.

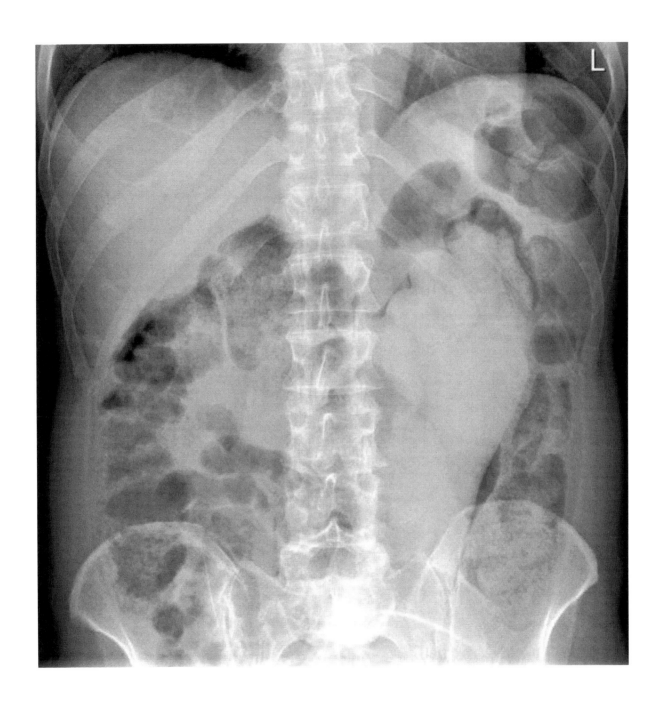

Fist Shaped Dildo

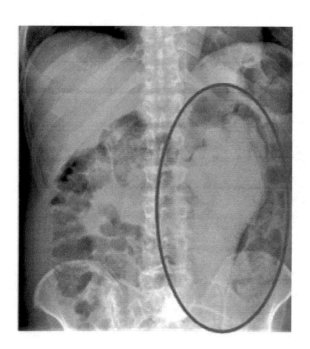

This guy presented with abdominal pain and a sheepish look on his face... Think the embarrassment would teach him a lesson? Nope. He returned to the same hospital 2 years later in the same predicament.

Case courtesy of Dr. Andrew Dixon Alfred Health / Imaging @ Olympic Park, Melbourne, Australia. Reprinted with permission from http://radiopaedia.org/cases/rectal-foreign-body-spleen-tickler.Toy fist image courtesy of www.sextoyodyssey.com.

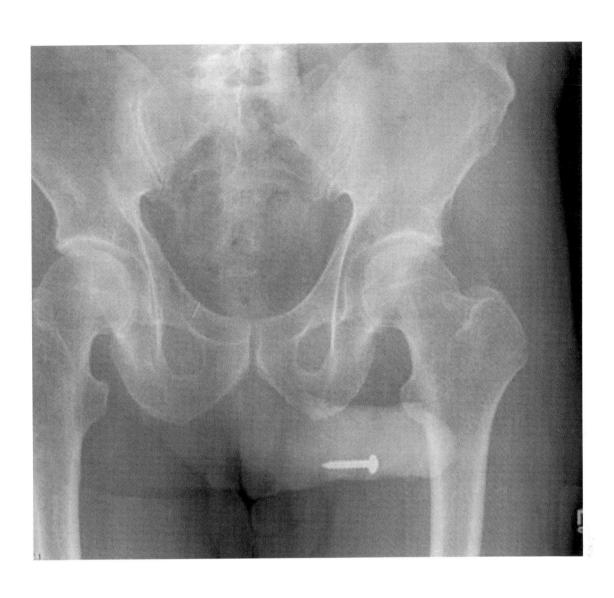

S.I.P.

S.I.P. was the indication provided by the ER doc to us in radiology for why they were ordering the x-ray. The medical field is full of acronyms. Often, in an effort to save time, these acronyms are included on x-ray orders. For example, every night I see M.V.A. (motor vehicle accident), F.B. (foreign body), R.D.S. (respiratory distress syndrome) to name a few, but I could not recall ever seeing S.I.P. before.

However, as soon as I hung the film up on the viewbox, the meaning became painfully obvious; screw... in ...

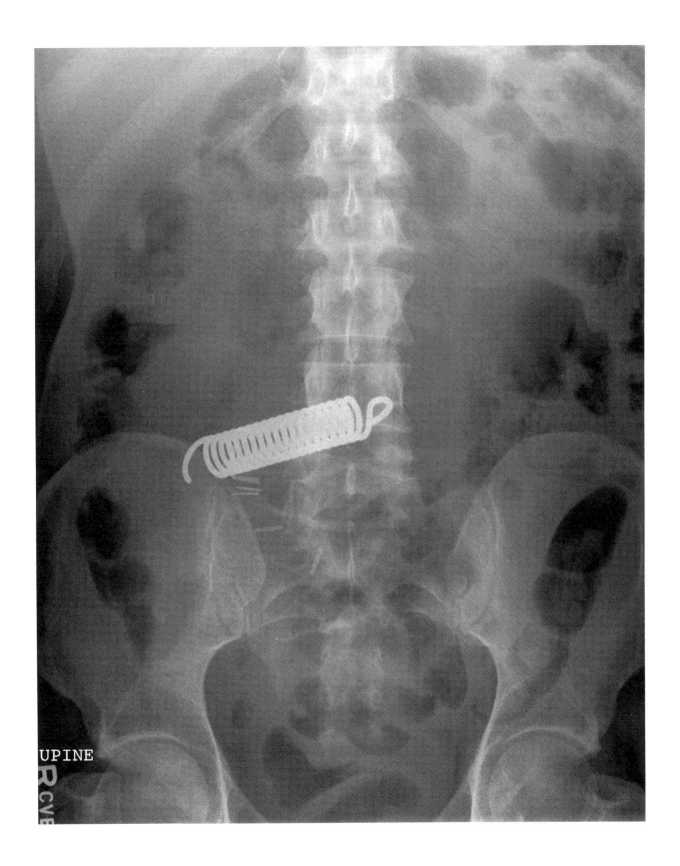

Spring

I don't know the real story, but here's what the patient told us; Having sex when a spring popped through the mattress, and against all odds, "sprung up into his anus". The spring had penetrated through bowel, and was freely floating in the abdominal cavity by the time he presented to the hospital. This required emergent surgery. You may have noticed clips in his pelvis. Those are from a prior surgery for a different foreign body.

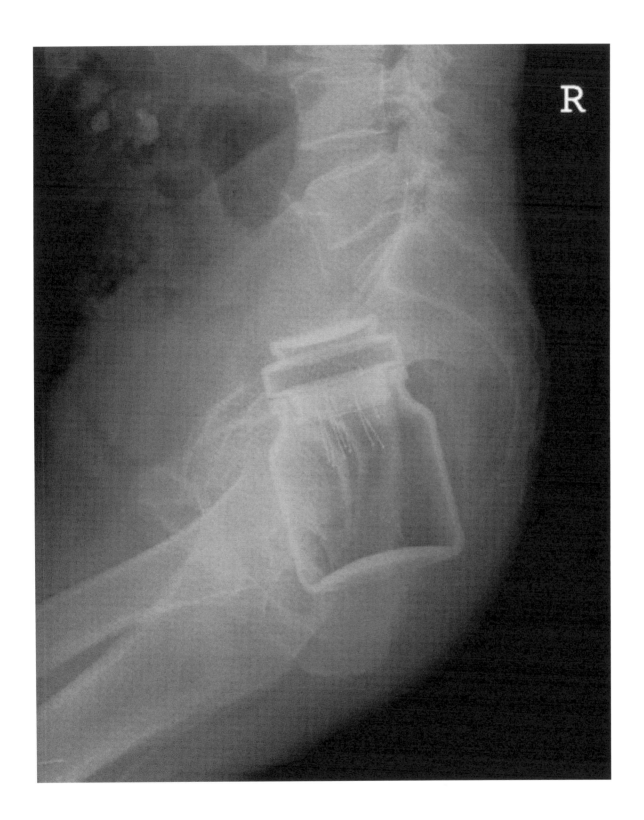

R

109

Instant Coffee

The best part of waking up, is Folgers© in your...what!?

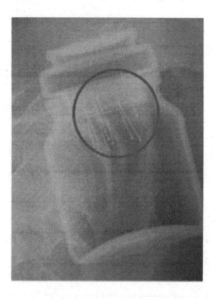

This patient was admitted, well, for obvious reasons. There are pins inserted in the inner rubber part of the lid of unknown significance.

Case courtesy of Dr. Frank Gaillard, Royal Melbourne Hospital, Melbourne, Australia. Reprinted with permission from http://radiopaedia.org/cases/rectal-foreign-body-instant-coffee-jar.

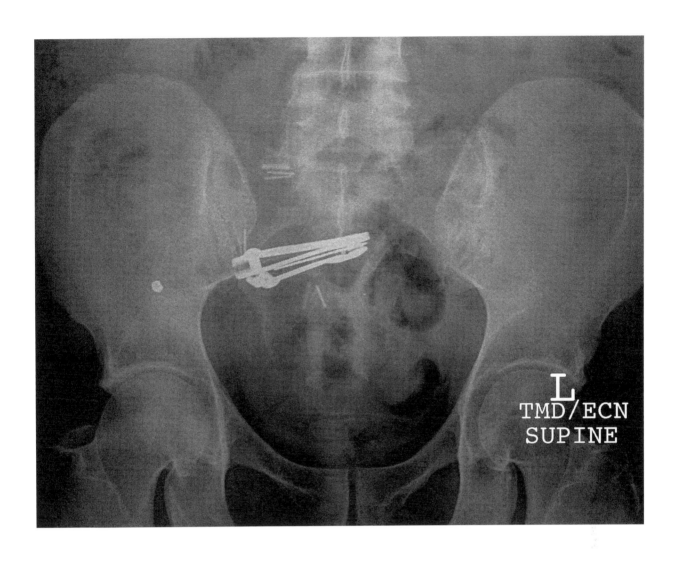

Toe-Nail Clippers

You cannot make this stuff up. When asked why he placed toe-nail clippers in his rectum, the patient stated, "I had finished clipping my nails". By the way, this was the same guy as the mattress spring case.

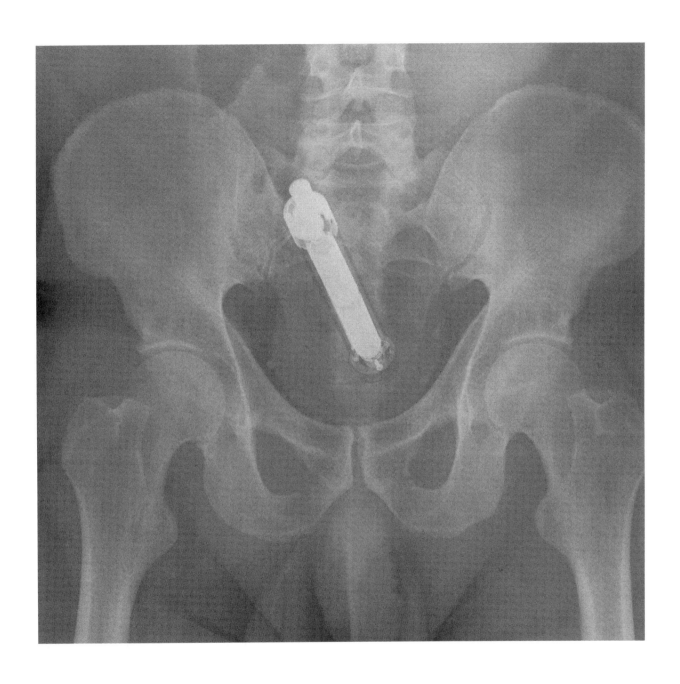

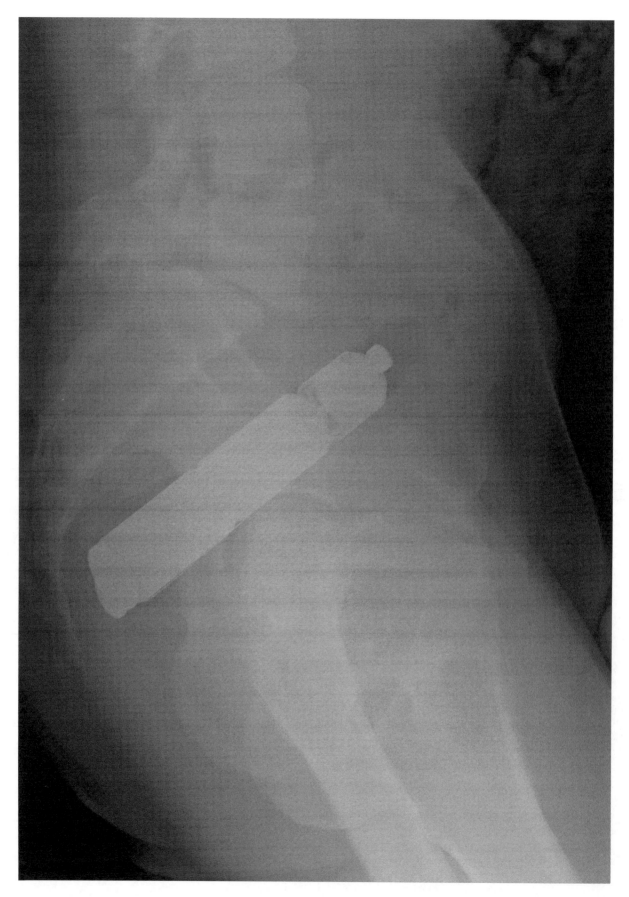

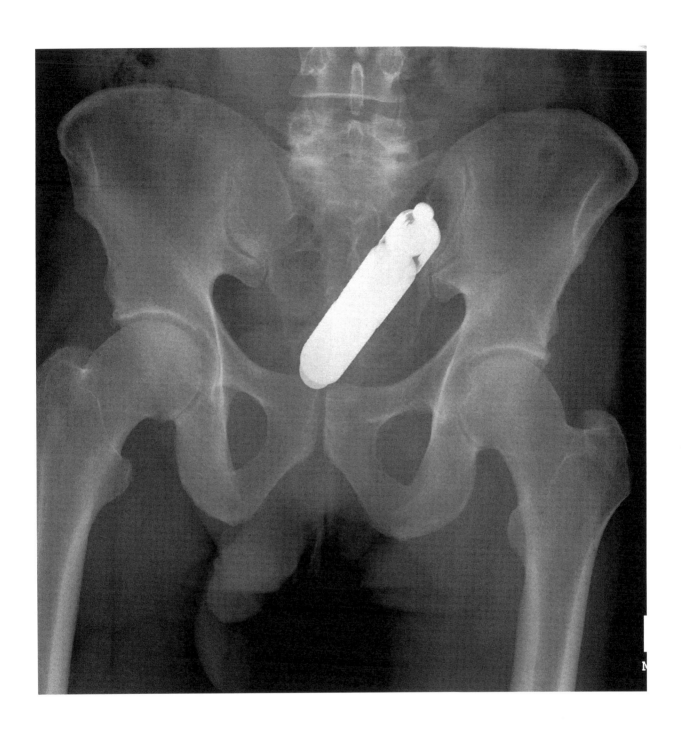

Vibrators

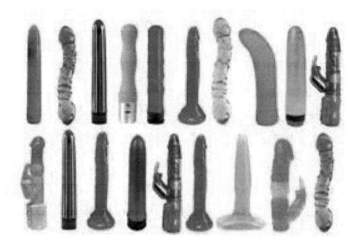

This happens relatively frequently. Anecdotally, the most common story is a married couple, and the object is most often "lost" in the male.

Despite the above cases being 3 different patients, they all used the same type of vibrator! Not sure if this is a particularly popular or slippery model, but it has resulted in multiple embarrassing trips to the ER.

Vibrators picture courtesy of The Guardian. Photograph: PR shot http://www.guardian.co.uk/lifeandstyle/2012/sep/07/how-the-vibrator-caused-buzz

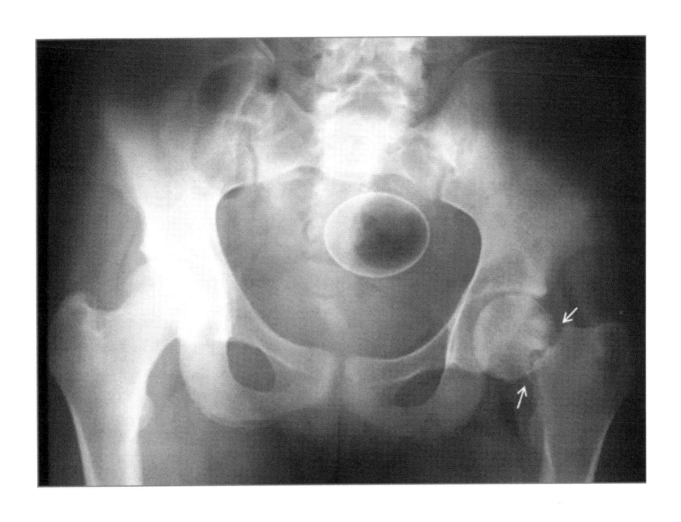

Egg

The incredible, edible, egg; apparently not just for breakfast anymore.

Inserting an egg into the rectum was used for palliative treatment in the small Iranian village where this patient was from. In this case, the "treatment" was likely being used to alleviate hip pain (note the unhealed left hip fracture (arrows).

Case courtesy of Dr. Saeed Rad and Dr. Mohammad.T Niknejad, Tabriz University of Medical Sciences, Tabriz, Iran. Reprinted with permission from http://radiopaedia.org/cases/rectal-foreign-body-egg.

THE END?

Are you a health care provider or patient with a particularly interesting foreign body x-ray and story? Send an email to foreignbodyxrays@gmail.com. If your x-ray is included in the 2nd edition, you'll receive a $50 gift card to the e-book store of your choosing!

Made in the USA
Columbia, SC
07 December 2018